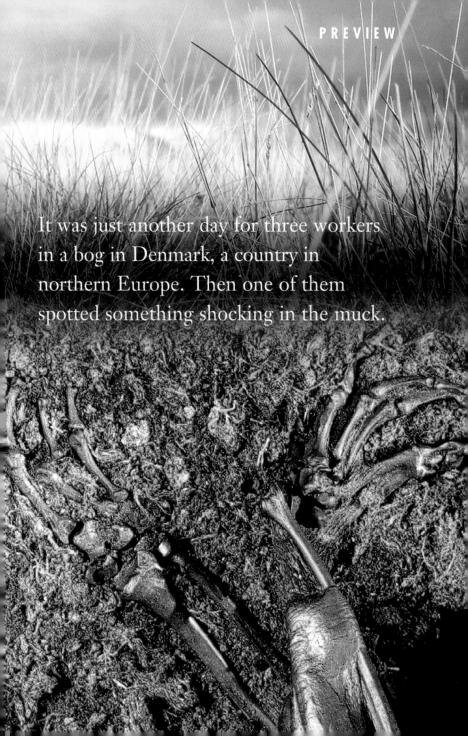

It was just another day for three workers in a bog in Denmark, a country in northern Europe. Then one of them spotted something shocking in the muck.

Murder Victim Uncovered?

It was a human face! Had the workers uncovered a murder victim? Stunned, they called the police.

To the workers' surprise, the police called in experts from the local museum. Apparently, this wasn't the first body to turn up in a bog. And museum experts had investigated those bodies as well.

The Investigation

The experts arrived at the bog. They gently
removed dirt from the body. It was a man.
He looked peaceful, as if he were resting.
But investigators would soon discover that
the man had been in the bog for a long time.
And he hadn't died peacefully.

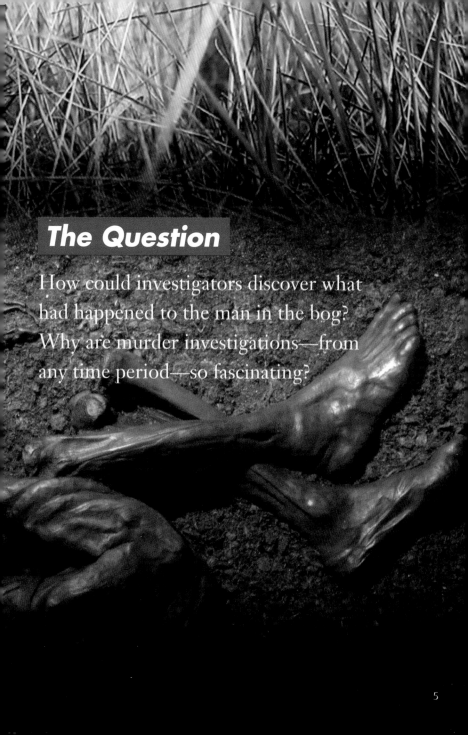

The Question

How could investigators discover what
had happened to the man in the bog?
Why are murder investigations—from
any time period—so fascinating?

PREVIEW PHOTOS

PAGES 1-5: Tollund Man is a 2,400-year-old bog body that was discovered in 1950. In these photos only the mummy's head is original.

Photographs ©: cover ditch: The Irish Image Collection/Design Pics/Science Source; cover grass: kotangens/iStockphoto; cover trees: Andreas Jakel/Imagebroker/Shutterstock; cover mummy: Christophe Boisvieux/Getty Images; 1 top: AntoMale/Shutterstock; 1 bottom: Carlos Muñoz-Yagüe/Science Source; 2-3: Christophe Boisvieux/Getty Images; 4-5: Silkeborg Museum, Denmark; 7 ditch: The Irish Image Collection/Design Pics/Science Source; 7 grass: kotangens/iStockphoto; 7 trees: Andreas Jakel/Imagebroker/Shutterstock; 7 mummy: Christophe Boisvieux/Getty Images; 8: Carlos Muñoz-Yagüe/Science Source; 10: Tammy Fullum/iStockphoto; 12: Niels Tilsted Søndergaard; 13: National Museum of Denmark; 14: Carlos Muñoz-Yagüe/Science Source; 16: Carlos Muñoz-Yagüe/Science Source; 17: Carlos Muñoz-Yagüe/Science Source; 17 inset: Neil Fletcher & Matthew Ward/Getty Images; 18-19: Christian Jegou/Publiphoto/Science Source; 18 inset: S. Vannini/De Agostini/Getty Images; 20: Philippe Froesch/Silkeborg Museum, Denmark; 23: Silkeborg Museum, Denmark; 24-25: Rógvi N. Johansen, Photo/media Moesgaard; 26: Digital Motion/National Geographic Creative; 28: National Museum of Denmark; 30: Niels Bach; 32: National Museum of Denmark; 33 top: James P. Blair/National Geographic Creative; 33 bottom: Glen H. Doran/Florida State University; 34: William West/AFP/Getty Images; 35: Carlos Muñoz-Yagüe/Science Source; 36 left: Paula Burch/Tulane University; 36-37: Ira Block/National Geographic Creative; 38 left: Slonov/iStockphoto; 38 center: simonkr/iStockphoto; 38 right: rj lerich/Shutterstock; 38 bottom: Chromakey/Shutterstock; 39 top left: jamesbenet/iStockphoto; 39 center: majkel/iStockphoto; 39 top right: elnavegante/Shutterstock; 39 bottom paper: jane/iStockphoto; 39 bottom ruler: Kitch Bain/Shutterstock; 40 top: julio donoso/Sygma/Getty Images; 40 center: Maria Stenzel/National Geographic Creative; 40 bottom: William A. Allard/National Geographic Creative; 42 qarqan: Toru Yamanaka/AFP/Getty Images; 42 pompeii: Sean Sexton Collection/Bridgeman Images; 42 otzi: Sean Sexton Collection/Bridgeman Images; 42 maggie: George Frey/Getty Images.

Library of Congress Cataloging-in-Publication Data
Names: Grace, N. B., author.
Title: Mummies and murder : bodies in the swamp / N. B. Grace.
Other titles: Mummies unwrapped!
Description: [New edition] | New York, NY : Scholastic Inc., 2020. | Series: Xbooks | First published as: Mummies unwrapped! New York : Franklin Watts, 2008. | Includes index. | Audience: Grades 4-6, (provided by Scholastic Inc.)
Identifiers: LCCN 2019029899| ISBN 9780531238141 (library binding) | ISBN 9780531243800 (paperback)
Subjects: LCSH: Mummies--Juvenile literature. | Bog bodies--Juvenile literature. | Embalming--Juvenile literature.
Classification: LCC GN293 .G73 2020 | DDC 393/.3--dc23

Printed in Johor Bahru, Malaysia   108

SCHOLASTIC, XBOOKS, and associated logos are trademarks and/or registered trademarks of Scholastic Inc.

1 2 3 4 5 6 7 8 9 10 R 29 28 27 26 25 24 23 22 21 20

Scholastic Inc., 557 Broadway, New York, NY 10012.

MUMMIES AND MURDER

Bodies in the Swamp

N.B. GRACE

 SCHOLASTIC

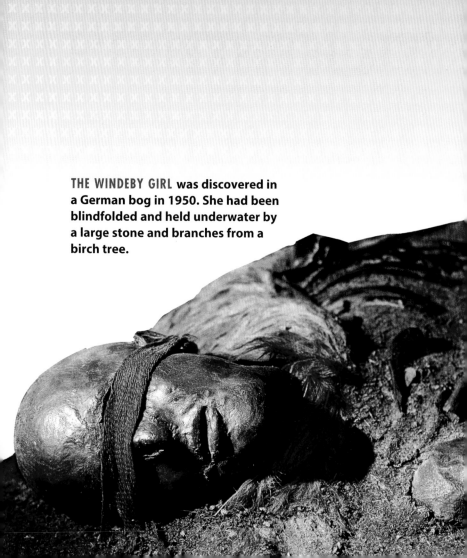

THE WINDEBY GIRL was discovered in a German bog in 1950. She had been blindfolded and held underwater by a large stone and branches from a birch tree.

PEAT BOGS are wetlands where layers of dead plant material form a dense soil called peat.

1

The Face in the Swamp

It was just another day of work...
until something unexpected turned up.

Brothers Emil and Viggo Hojgaard had a really dirty job. And on one day in 1950, digging in a bog would turn up something really shocking.

Early in the morning, the two men and Viggo's wife, Grethe, headed out to work in a bog near the village of Tollund, Denmark. Bogs, like swamps, are soft, wet areas of ground. They can be dark and eerie. Many legends have been written about them. People

VIGGO AND GRETHE HOJGAARD
**stand in the peat bog where
they uncovered a bog body.**

used to believe that trolls and spirits lurked in bogs, waiting to prey on innocent travelers.

Beware of Bogs

In fact, bogs *can* be dangerous. People can lose their footing, get sucked into the ooze, and drown. And long ago, people were sometimes killed and then thrown into the muck!

On this particular day, the Hojgaards were cutting peat. That's a type of dense soil made of rotted plants. They dug into the ground with shovels and then cut the peat into bricks. The bricks would later be dried and burned for fuel.

Suddenly, Grethe noticed something in the muck. It was a human face!

GRETHE HOJGAARD **spotted this face while digging in the bog.**

THE BOG BODY was found with a rope tied around his neck.

2

A Strangled Corpse

Digging up
a gruesome mystery.

Had the Hojgaards uncovered a murder victim?
They called the police.

When the police heard that a body had been
found in a bog, they contacted a local museum.
The police weren't sure whether the man had been
murdered. But they suspected that if he had been, it
wasn't recently. Two ancient bodies had been found
in the bog years earlier.

The police and the museum experts joined the Hojgaards at the bog. The experts from the museum would take over the investigation.

They carefully uncovered the body of a small man. He had a well-preserved face. And he looked as if he were sleeping. But as the experts brushed away bits of dirt from the man's body, they discovered something shocking. He had a rope tied around his neck!

Workers gently removed the body, placed it in a box, and took it to the museum. Scientists there confirmed that the body had been mummified, or preserved, in the bog. The Tollund Man, as he is now called, had been killed about 2,400 years before. Now they had to figure out why.

A BOG BODY called the Stidsholt Woman was found in a bog in Denmark in 1859.

Bog Mummies

Why don't bodies left in bogs decay? Scientists say there are three main reasons.

1. Running water takes in oxygen from the air. Living things such as plants, fish, and most bacteria need oxygen to survive. But the water in bogs is very still. It doesn't contain much oxygen. So in a bog there are few—if any—organisms that feed on bodies and cause them to decay.

2. Bogs contain a kind of acid released by plants. This acid preserves bodies much as vinegar preserves pickles.

3. Many bogs contain sphagnum, a kind of moss. This moss produces a chemical that can preserve a body. It also dyes bodies a deep, dark brown.

Sphagnum moss

The Other Mummies

The ancient Egyptians preserved the bodies of their dead—especially members of the royal families. They believed that the bodies and spirits would live again in the afterlife.

Here's how they made a mummy!

A STONE TOMB holds the gold-covered coffin of an ancient Egyptian pharaoh.

Removal of internal organs. Egyptians used a long, hooked wire to pull the brain through the nostrils. They removed other internal organs through a small cut in the abdomen. They did not remove the heart! It was believed to be the source of thought. The mummy would need it in the afterlife.

Dehydration. The body was covered with a substance called natron for 35 days. It drew all the moisture out of the body.

Coating and wrapping. The body was coated with resin and wrapped tightly in long strips of linen cloth.

Organ storage. The dehydrated internal organs were put in four containers called canopic jars.

Body storage in a coffin. If it was the body of a pharaoh, several golden coffins were used, placed one inside the other.

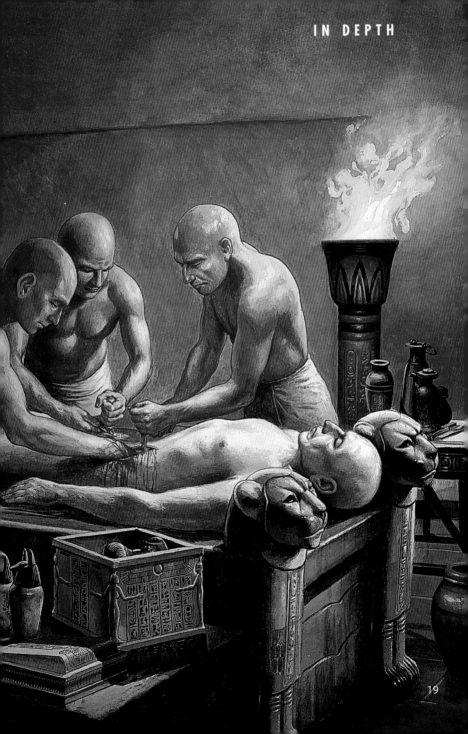

19

HERE'S A RECONSTRUCTION of what Tollund Man might have looked like when he was alive.

3

The Tollund Man Speaks

Scientists try to find out more about the Tollund Man.

The Tollund Man is in good company. Over the past few centuries, mummified human remains have been found in bogs all over northern Europe. Most of these remains were found by people who were cutting peat—just like the Hojgaards had been.

Some bog bodies are in better shape than others. Sometimes only body parts are uncovered. Other bog bodies are whole but very decayed.

The Tollund Man is one of the best-preserved bog bodies ever discovered. Archeologists—scientists who study past ways of life—were eager to get their hands on him. He was examined first in 1950 and then again in 2002.

Mummy Profile

Here's what scientists learned when they examined the Tollund Man.

- He died around 350 BCE.
- His wisdom teeth had come in, so he was at least 20 years old. Scientists think that he was probably closer to 40.
- He was at least 5'3" tall.
- He had scars on his feet that showed he walked barefoot some of the time.
- His last meal was soup. The soup contained barley with a fungus on it. Why was this fungus in the soup? Scientists think that it might have been added to the meal to make him unconscious before he was killed.

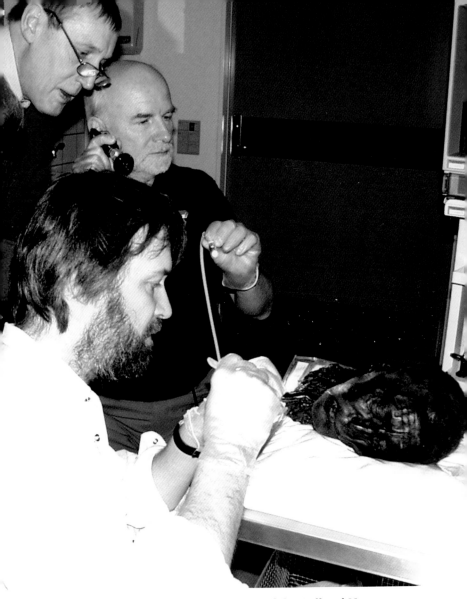

EXPERTS IN DENMARK examine the head of the Tollund Man. They found that his brain was very well preserved.

Grauballe Man

Was this mummy a murder victim, too?

Grauballe Man's body was found in a bog in Denmark. He was also a victim of a mysterious murder. His throat was slit from ear to ear. This mummy was so well preserved that his fingerprints could still be seen—2,300 years after he died!

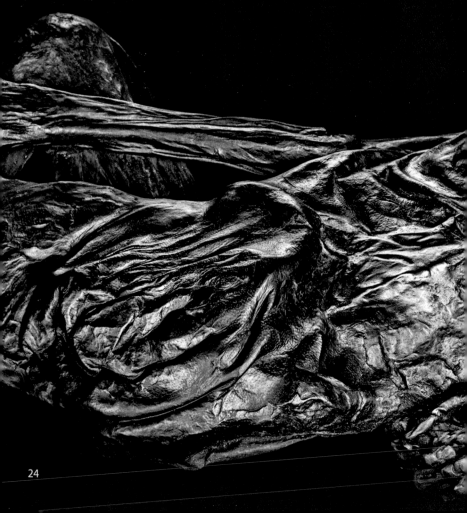

SCIENTISTS AGREE that the Tollund Man died by hanging, as this re-creation shows.

4

Mum(my)'s the Word

Was this murder part of a religious ritual?

Archeologists had learned a lot about the Tollund Man. But one question continued to haunt them. Why had he been killed? Scientists agreed that he'd been murdered. He had been hanged by the rope that was found around his neck. But why?

It wasn't the first time this question had come up. Many of the bog bodies that have been found over the centuries showed signs of violent deaths. Some, like the Tollund Man, had been hanged. Others had been strangled. Many had their throats cut. Some had been clubbed or stabbed. Several bodies were cut into parts.

There were other surprising things about the bodies. Some were wearing clothes, but others were naked. One was blindfolded. Numerous bodies were found weighed down with boulders. And a few had been tied down or pinned by branches so they couldn't get away.

ELLING WOMAN

The Mummy Next Door

One of these bodies is now known as the Elling Woman. She was the Tollund Man's neighbor. The Elling Woman was found 12 years before Tollund Man. She was buried just 260 feet away from where he was discovered. A farmer had been digging for peat in the bog when his shovel struck her body.

Elling Woman's body was not as well preserved as the Tollund Man's. Still, experts could tell that she too had been hanged. And she had been buried with care. She had been placed on her side in a grave in the peat. And a blanket had been wrapped around her feet.

Bog Burial

How did all these bodies end up in bogs? It wasn't by accident. Some scientists think that the bodies might have been placed in bogs after they were executed for being criminals or outcasts.

Had the Tollund Man committed a crime thousands of years ago—and paid with his life? Maybe.

Or perhaps there's another explanation for his murder.

Some experts believe that the Tollund Man may have been killed as part of a religious ritual. In some religions, animals are sacrificed in the hope of pleasing a god or goddess. Some ancient religions even

THE TOLLUND MAN'S BODY was probably carefully placed in a grave dug into the peat.

sacrificed humans. Is this what happened to the Tollund Man?

Roman Diaries

Unfortunately, it's impossible to say whether the Tollund Man was sacrificed in a religious ritual or punished for a crime. People who lived in the area at the time of his death didn't leave written records.

But there are some clues. One clue comes from ancient Romans who traveled to these lands. They wrote down what they learned during their travels.

According to the Romans, people in northern Europe would offer human sacrifices to their gods. Perhaps the people who killed Tollund Man wanted the gods to bring them a good harvest or warm weather.

Another clue is the way the Tollund Man was placed in the bog.

Experts point out that his body was handled carefully. It was not treated like a criminal's would have been. His corpse wasn't carelessly thrown into the bog. Instead, the Tollund Man had been placed

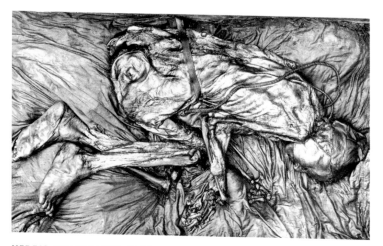

HERE'S THE TOLLUND MAN shortly after he was discovered.

gently in a grave dug into the peat. He was laid on his side, with his legs bent against his stomach. Scientists also think that his eyelids and mouth were closed after he died.

Did this careful treatment indicate something special about the Tollund Man?

Scientists don't know for certain. But they do know that a man who walked barefoot and was about 5'3" was murdered over 2,000 years ago. And his body was placed in a bog. He ate soup before he died.

But why was he killed? That's still a mystery. **X**

Backyard Bog Bodies

There are bog bodies in the United States, too.

Bog mummies aren't found only in Europe. The bodies of ancient Native Americans have been discovered in marshes in the southeastern United States.

At Windover Pond, near Titusville, Florida, a worker stumbled on a gravesite in an ancient bog. It was found to hold the remains of nearly 200 bodies. And almost half of the bodies contained well-preserved brains! Archeologists from Florida State University have dated the bodies to about 7,000 years ago.

THIS JAWBONE was found at the Titusville site.

Mummy's Furry Friend

People in ancient Egypt really loved their cats. And they didn't want to go to the afterlife without them. So some ancient Egyptians mummified their pets. Here's a cat that has gotten the royal treatment.

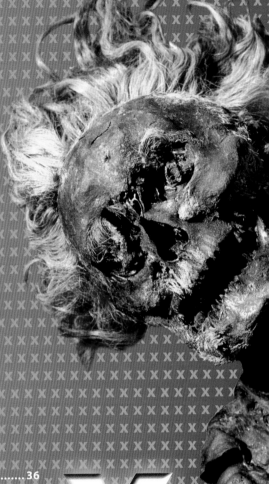

X FILES

Ancient Ink

Anthropologist John Verano unwraps an ancient woman warrior.

JOHN VERANO is a professor of anthropology at Tulane University. He says an anthropologist needs "an interest in adventure and travel" and "a sense of curiosity!"

You worked with the mummy of a woman warrior found in Peru. What was your role?

DR. JOHN VERANO: I went to Peru when they were ready to take [the mummy] out of the ground. I observed as they unwrapped the body in the lab. It took two months. It was a very complicated mummy. There were several bundles wrapped one inside the other with hundreds of yards of cotton.

The woman warrior was buried with war clubs and jewelry. Why?

VERANO: War clubs could be symbols of power. Or it

could be that [people] gave her weapons for protection in the afterlife. She also has a necklace of human heads made in gold. We think she was high-ranking because of all the beautiful objects buried with her and because she was buried near the top of a pyramid.

What else was interesting about this mummy?

VERANO: She had tattoos. There are spiders, crabs, worms, and mythical creatures on her right arm.

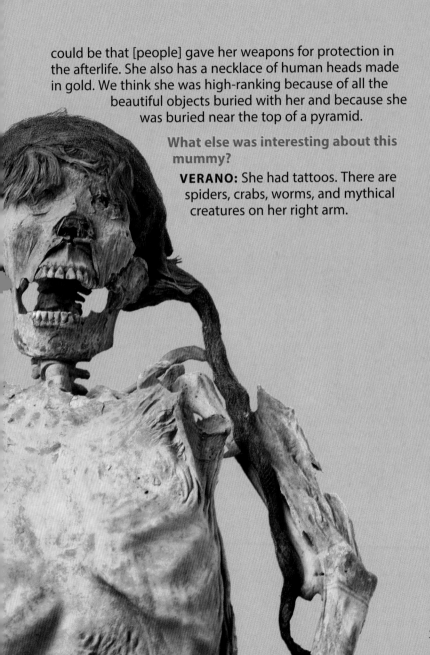

Measuring Mummies

Check out some of the tools of the trade used by anthropologists and archeologists.

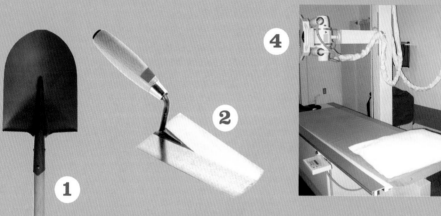

1

4

2

1 Shovel
Archeologists use shovels to remove dirt. They're used only when there aren't many artifacts in the area that might be damaged or broken.

2 Trowel This is the most common tool at a dig site. It is used to slowly and carefully remove dirt, one layer at a time.

3 Microscope
Archeologists use this to look at things that can't easily be seen by the naked eye.

4 X-ray machine
These machines use radiation to take photos of the bones inside a mummy.

3

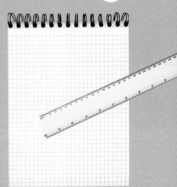

5 CT scanner
This creates a three-dimensional image of the inside of the body.

Once something is taken out of the ground, you can't re-create how it was found!

6 Camera, notebook, and pen
Archeologists use these to record what is found at the site. They must keep exact records.

7 Graph paper and ruler These are used for making a detailed map of the site. Some scientists also use GPS and other digital tools for this purpose.

Here's a selection
of mummies from
around the world.

Meet th

Who?

Nazca child

Inca girl

**Italians
from the
Middle Ages**

Mummies!

Where and when mummified?	How?	What do we know?
Peru, about 1,500 years ago	Buried in sand that is rich in salt and nitrates, which preserved the body	The Nazca culture thrived in Peru between 300 BCE and 800 CE. Their dead were usually buried in a fetal position.
Northern Argentina, 500 years ago	Naturally frozen and buried under several feet of rock and dirt	The Inca Empire ruled north-western Peru from 1438 to 1533. This Inca girl was one of three child mummies found on a burial platform. She was between eight and 15 years old, and was probably left as a sacrifice to the gods.
Palermo, Italy, about 400 years ago	Dehydrated on racks, then washed with vinegar. Some were embalmed.	Priests in a monastery mummified a monk. So the locals decided to preserve their loved ones, too. But they had to pay for upkeep or the bodies would be removed from the catacomb where they were stored.

Qarqan baby

Citizen from Pompeii

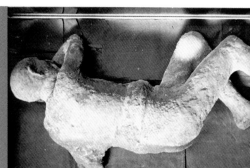

Otzi the Iceman

Maggie

Where and when mummified?	How?	What do we know?
China, between 5 BCE and 3 CE	Mummified by humans, then buried in a tomb	The baby's eyes were covered with stone chips, and her face was masked with cloth. Her mouth was sealed with gold foil and flour paste, and her nose was plugged with wool.
Italy, 79 CE	Buried in volcanic ash and debris	The ancient Roman city of Pompeii was wiped out by a volcano. The dead were covered in ash. Over time, the ash hardened around the bodies. The bodies eventually decayed.
The Alps, between Austria and Italy, about 3300 BCE	Frozen in ice	Some scientists think Otzi was hunting when he and his companions got into a fight with a rival group. After losing a lot of blood, Otzi carefully put down his equipment, lay down, and died.
Salt Lake City, Utah, 1996	Cast in bronze	Sue Menu couldn't bear to part with her dead poodle, Maggie. So Menu paid $27,000 to have Maggie mummified and bronzed.

Here's a selection of books and websites for more information about mummies and bog bodies.

What to Read Next

NONFICTION

Barber, Nicola. *Tomb Explorers.* Chicago: Raintree, 2013.

Cleveland-Peck, Patricia. *The Secrets of Tutankhamun: Egypt's Boy King and His Incredible Tomb.* New York: Bloomsbury Children's Books, 2018.

Eamer, Claire. *Out of the Ice: How Climate Change Is Revealing the Past.* Toronto: Kids Can Press, 2018.

Getz, David. *Frozen Girl: The Discovery of an Incan Mummy.* New York: Square Fish, 2018.

Grace, N. B. *Mummies Unwrapped! The Science of Mummy-Making.* New York: Franklin Watts, 2008.

Hollihan, Kerrie Logan. *Mummies Exposed!* (Creepy and True). New York: Abrams, 2019.

Huey, Lois Miner. *Children of the Past: Archaeology and the Lives of Kids.* New York: Millbrook Press, 2017.

Hynson, Colin. *You Wouldn't Want to Be an Inca Mummy!* New York: Scholastic, 2008.

Prior, Natalie Jane. *The Encyclopedia of Preserved People: Pickled, Frozen, and Mummified Corpses from Around the World.* New York: Crown Publishers, 2003.

Putnam, James. *Mummy* (DK Eyewitness Books). New York: DK Publishing, 2004.

Sloan, Christopher. *Mummies: Dried, Tanned, Sealed, Drained, Frozen, Embalmed, Stuffed, Wrapped, and Smoked . . . and We're Dead Serious.* Washington, D.C.: National Geographic Children's Books, 2010.

Wilcox, Charlotte. *Bog Mummies: Preserved in Peat.* Mankato MN: Capstone Press, 2006.

FICTION

Bosch, Pseudonymous. *You Have to Stop This* (The Secret Series, Book 5). New York: Little, Brown Books for Young Readers, 2012.

Dowd, Siobhan. *Bog Child*. New York: David Fickling Books, 2010.

Evans, Malayna. *Jagger Jones and the Mummy's Ankh*. Raleigh, North Carolina: Month9Books, 2019.

LaFevers, R. L. *Theodosia and the Last Pharaoh*. New York: Houghton Mifflin, 2011.

Narayan, Natasha. *The Mummy Snatcher of Memphis* (A Kit Salter Adventure). New York: Quercus, 2010.

Poe, Edgar Allan. "Some Words with a Mummy" from *Great Short Works of Edgar Allan Poe*. New York: Harper Perennial, 1970.

Stine, R. L. *The Dummy Meets the Mummy!* (Goosebumps SlappyWorld #8). New York: Scholastic, 2019.

Van de Grier, Susan. *A Gift for Ampato*. Toronto, Canada: Groundwood Books, 1999.

Ward, Kaitlin. *Where She Fell*. New York: Scholastic Press, 2018.

GLOSSARY

anthropologist (an-thruh-POL-uh-jist) *noun* a person who studies the beliefs and lifestyles of different people around the world

anthropology (an-thruh-POL-uh-jee) *noun* the study of human beings, including their bones, language, and culture

archeologist (ar-kee-OL-uh-jist) *noun* a person who studies human history by digging up and examining ancient buildings, objects, and human remains

bacteria (bak-TEER-ee-ah) *noun* a type of single-celled life-form

bog (BAWG) *noun* an area of wet, marshy ground

catacombs (KAT-uh-kohms) *noun* underground passageways with holes in the walls for storing the dead

corpse (KORPS) *noun* a dead human body

decay (dee-KAY) *verb* to rot

dehydrated (dee-HYE-dray-tid) *adjective* having had the water removed from it

embalm (em-BAHLM) *verb* to preserve a body after death, a process developed by the ancient Egyptians

execute (EK-suh-kyoot) *verb* to kill someone as a punishment for a crime

fetal position (FEE-tuhl puh-ZISH-uhn) *noun* the curled-up position of a fetus in the womb

foul play (FOWL PLAY) *noun* dishonest or violent behavior

mummy (MUH-mee) *noun* a dead body that has been preserved and has lasted a very long time

mythical (MITH-i-kuhl) *adjective* occurring in myths or folktales; imaginary or not real

natron (NAY-tron) *noun* a mixture of soda ash, baking soda, and salt that the ancient Egyptians used to dry out mummies

organism (OR-guh-niz-uhm) *noun* an individual animal, plant, or single-celled life-form

peat (PEET) *noun* dark brown, partially decayed plant matter that is found in bogs and swamps; peat can be burned for fuel

pharaoh (FAIR-oh) *noun* the title of kings in ancient Egypt

preserve (prih-ZURV) *verb* to protect something so that it doesn't change or decay

remains (ri-MAYNZ) *noun* part of something that was once alive

resin (REZ-in) *noun* a yellow or brown sticky substance that oozes from pine trees and many other plants

ritual (RICH-oo-uhl) *noun* a set of actions performed repeatedly as part of a religious ceremony or social custom

sacrifice (SAK-ruh-fisse) *verb* to kill a living thing and offer it to a god

sphagnum (SFAG-nuhm) *noun* a type of moss that grows on top of bogs

unconscious (uhn-KON-shuhss) *adjective* not awake; not able to see, feel, or think

INDEX

METRIC CONVERSIONS

Feet to meters: 1 ft is about 0.3 m
Miles to kilometers: 1 mi is about 1.6 km
Pounds to kilograms: 1 lb is about 0.45 kg
Ounces to grams: 1 oz is about 28 g